I am Jim Henson

BRAD MELTZER

illustrated by Christopher Eliopoulos

 DIAL BOOKS FOR YOUNG READERS

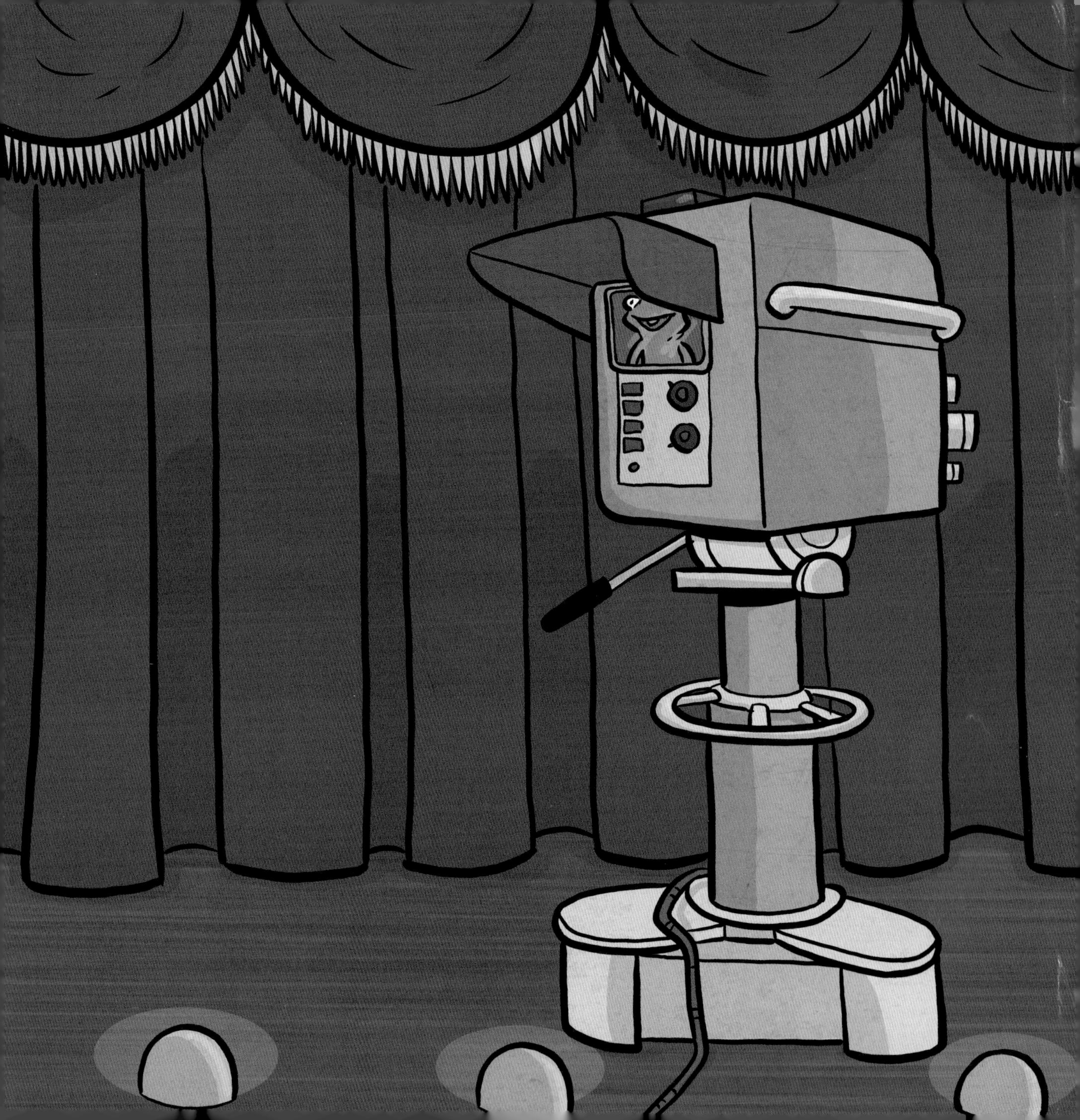

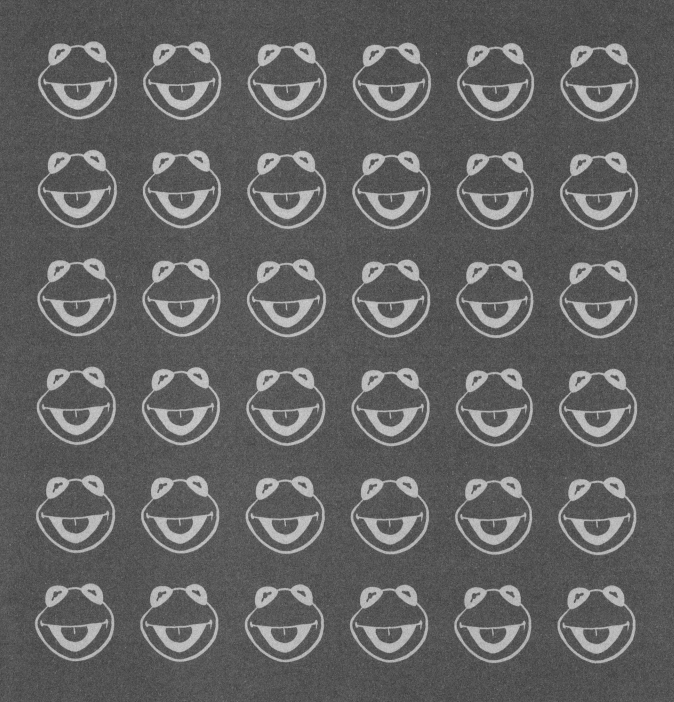

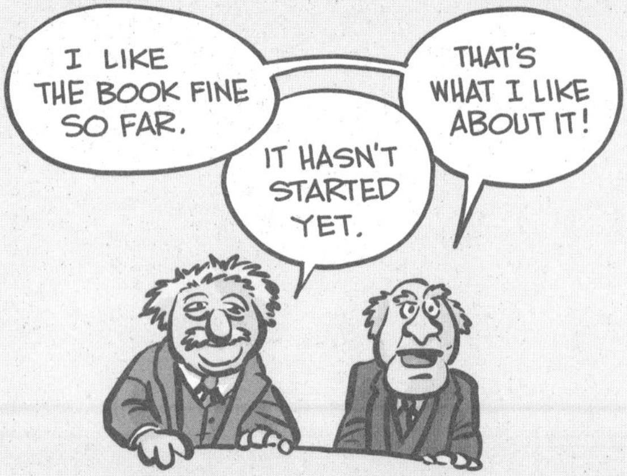
I LIKE THE BOOK FINE SO FAR.
IT HASN'T STARTED YET.
THAT'S WHAT I LIKE ABOUT IT!

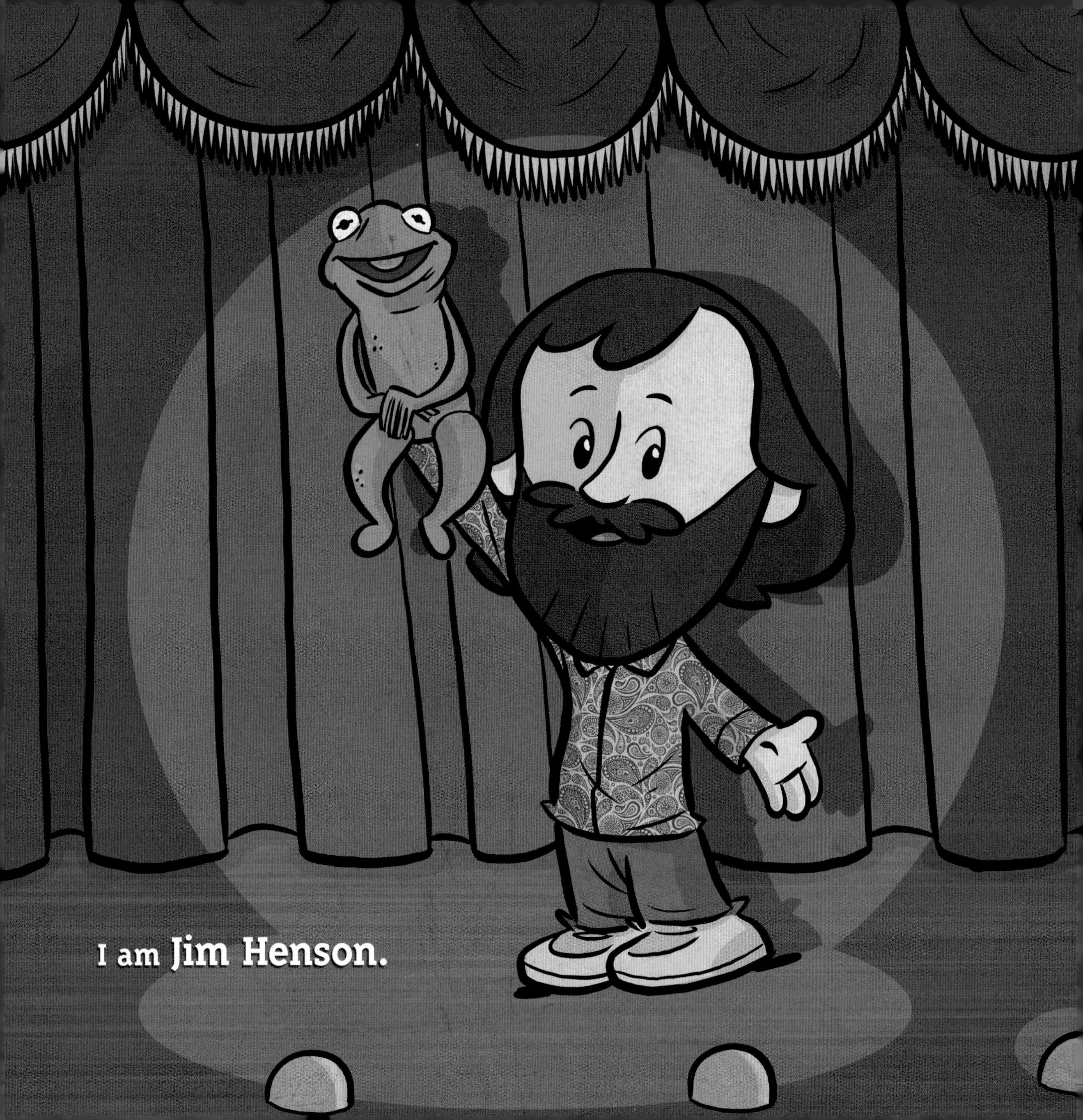

I am **Jim Henson.**

Oh, good. You're here.

What's the fun of a story if you don't have anyone to share it with?

Growing up in Mississippi, I used to love to watch birds.

I even made my own book, where I'd list each bird I saw and add my own drawings.

THAT BIRD UP THERE IS MY FAVORITE— THE BLACKBIRD.

BLACKBIRDS HAVE FUN PERSONALITIES, AND I ALSO LOVE THEIR OTHER NAME:

THE GRACKLE.

DON'T YOU JUST LOVE FUNNY NAMES LIKE THAT?

My whole life, I've loved kooky words.

Wanna know what else I loved? Laughing.

As a kid, this was one of my favorite family jokes.

My mom used to play it on my brother and me.

SAY WHEN.

GEE, THAT'S ENOUGH.

MOM, THAT'S ENOUGH!

MOM!

YOU DIDN'T SAY "WHEN."

At eight years old, I'd come here: to the movie theater.
Every Saturday, this was my favorite place.

For fifteen cents I could get a bag of popcorn and spend the whole day watching cartoons, newsreels, action movies, and comedies.

My favorites were the ones with wild clothing and far-off locations, like the Old West or foreign countries.

The rest of the week, my friends and I would re-create what we saw in the movies, using homemade props and costumes.

With a little imagination, we'd start pretending.
There was no limit to what we could create.

My grandparents played a big role in my life.

I got my middle name—Maury—from my grandfather, who loved to laugh too. But he never laughed *at* anyone, never made fun of people.

As for my grandmother, she was my best audience.

When she came over to visit, we'd use paint, glue, and crayons to make the most amazing art projects.

She was the one who encouraged me to draw things that made me happy: monsters with giant mouths and birds with big eyes.

Those days with my grandmother changed my life.
She encouraged me to tell stories.
She supported my love of reading.
And she was amazing with a needle and thread.
She could sew anything.

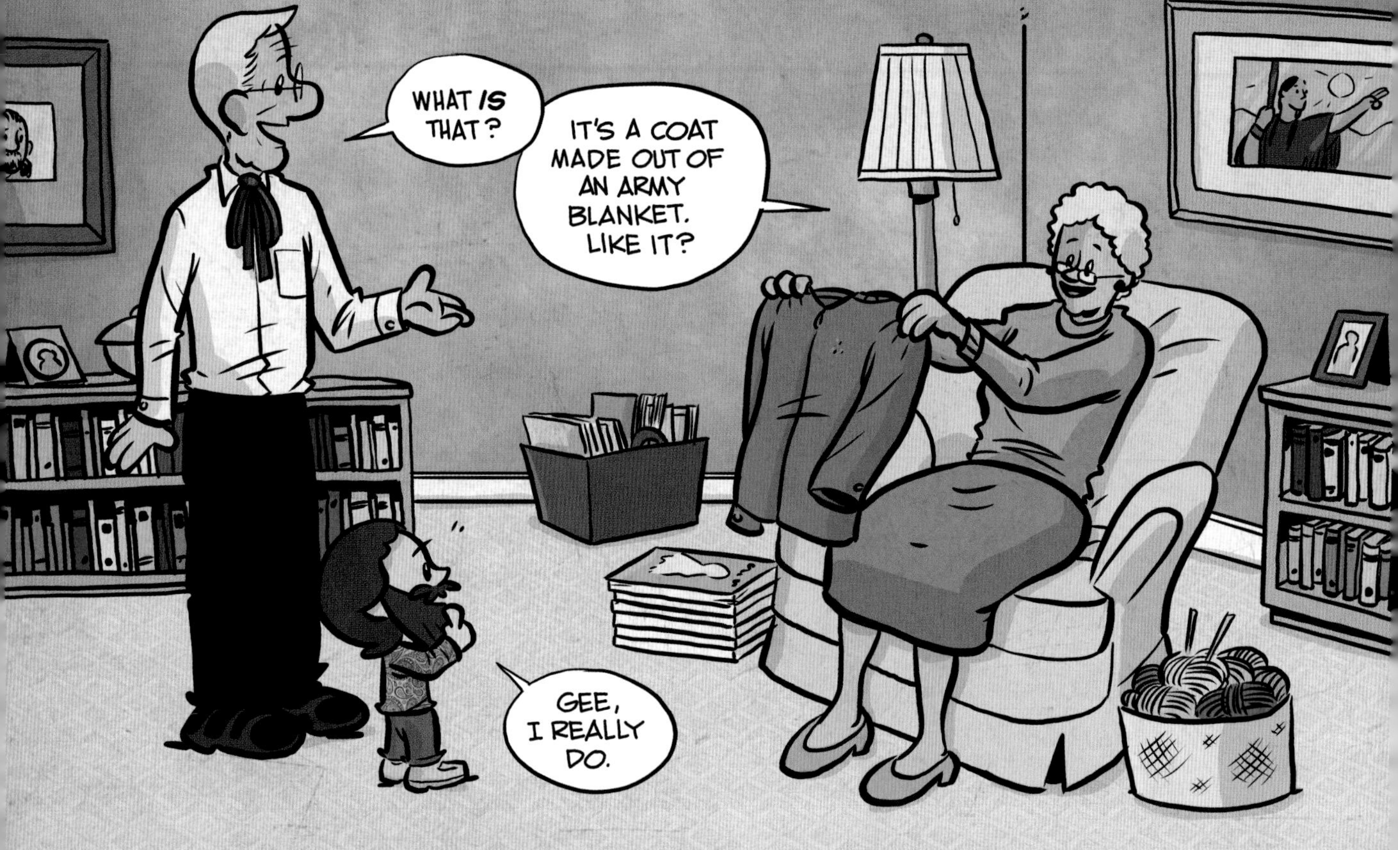
WHAT *IS* THAT?
IT'S A COAT MADE OUT OF AN ARMY BLANKET. LIKE IT?
GEE, I REALLY DO.

But the most important thing she taught me was that with my imagination, I could do anything. I could *be* anything, including. . .

A performer.

One night, during a skit in Cub Scouts, I had one of my friends stand in front of everyone with his hands behind his back.

Then I put my own hands in and. . .

I can still hear the crowd laughing.

I always loved a good performance.

Growing up, I listened to shows on the radio, like *Green Hornet*, *The Shadow*, and one of my favorite comedians, a ventriloquist named Edgar Bergen.

Even though Edgar Bergen did the voices, I never thought Charlie McCarthy or his other characters were puppets.

They were human to me.

His work was magic. Magic in the real sense: It seemed impossible.
That's what magic is. It creates wonder. It creates dreams that inspire.
I'd seen their pictures in newspapers. But here, with each
show . . . an ordinary object came to life.

Something happened when Edgar spoke through Charlie.
The puppeteer wasn't just sharing jokes. He was sharing
the best parts of himself.
And people were listening.

When I was thirteen, a new technology changed my life. At a friend's house, I saw an invention called...

I wouldn't give up.
Soon, my parents gave in.

On TV, I found comedians like Sid Caesar, Milton Berle, and Jack Benny. One of my favorites was Ernie Kovacs, who tilted the set and camera so everything slid sideways.

I especially loved variety shows, which had big casts that would sing, dance, and do comedy.

And there was *Kukla, Fran and Ollie*, a show where puppets made jokes and sang with a human costar.

The way they talked to each other—it was like those puppets were *alive*.

Right away, I knew one thing: I wanted to work in television.

At sixteen years old, I went looking for a job at all the local TV stations.

They all said no.
But like the time I begged my dad for a TV, I never gave up.

Soon after, a local station announced it was looking for a puppeteer.
I'd never used a puppet before, but my whole life, I loved creating.
This was the job I wanted. So how'd I get it?
The same way you get any dream: hard work.
I went to my high school library, took out books
on puppetry, built a few puppets, and went back to
the station.

They gave me a chance.
That was all I needed.

Was my first show a success?

No. It was canceled.

But did I give up? Not a chance.

My partner and I continued creating—continued working hard—and eventually we got our own five minutes before *The Tonight Show*.

Along the way, we came up with a name for our characters.

We called them Muppets, playing around with the word *puppet*.

But really, it was just a fun word.

Like grackle.

Our show was called *Sam and Friends*.
We needed a new puppet, and the answer was right in plain sight.

I WAS EIGHTEEN YEARS OLD AND FOUND MY MOTHER'S OLD WOOL COAT.

I CUT IT APART AND SEWED A NEW BODY.

MY GRANDMOTHER TAUGHT ME THAT ONE.

I gave it a pointed face.
I glued on the halves of a Ping-Pong ball for eyes.
And then I became the one who performed his voice.

Yes, he was turquoise back then. He wasn't even a frog. But he did have a name.
Kermit.

With each show, I kept inventing new characters,
dreaming up new ways to make people laugh.
On TV, unlike a puppet stage, there were no walls.
So we could film our Muppets from far away.

Or bring them really close for an easy laugh.

And while old-fashioned puppets had frozen expressions, our Muppets' faces could move. We could do faces that were funny . . . angry . . . or even sad.

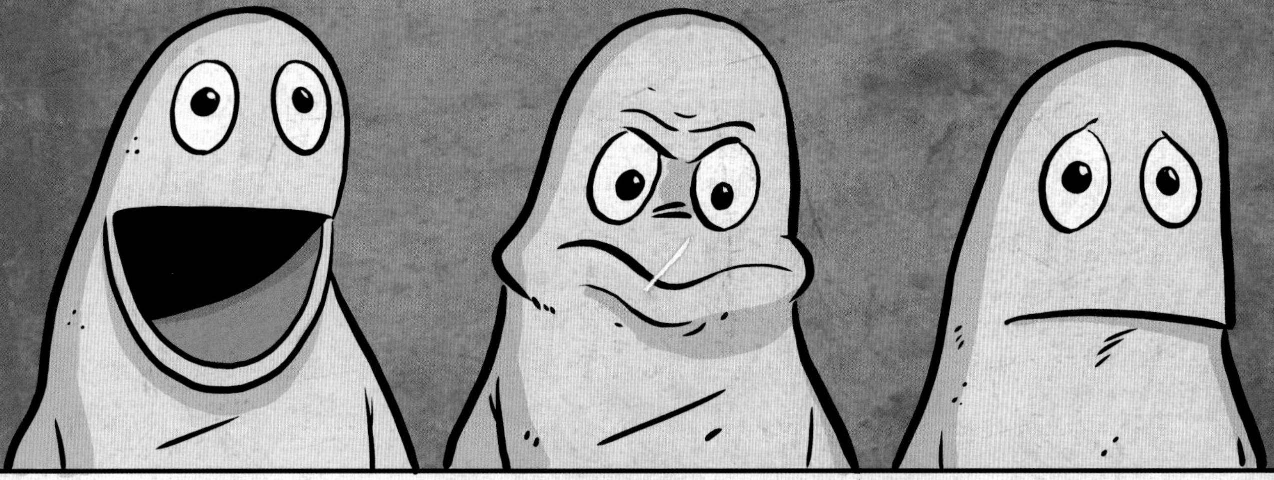

To make our Muppets seem even more real, we crossed their eyes slightly. This gave them focus.

Now they started to come *alive*.

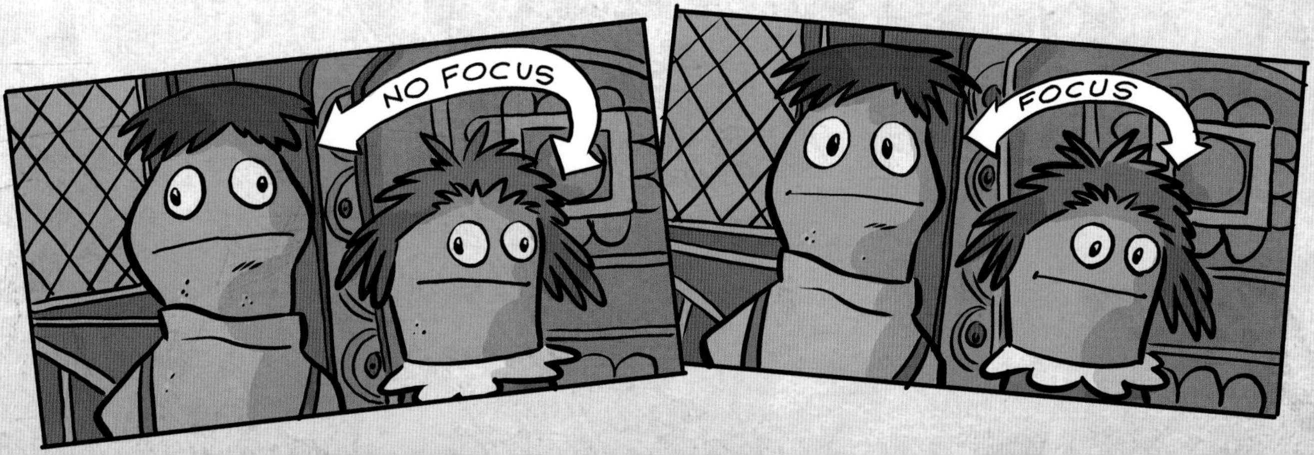
NO FOCUS
FOCUS

But do you want to know my real secret? Practice.

We would practice in a mirror, over and over, until it was just right.

The only way people would feel a sense of wonder was if we could give each character a life of its own.

LET'S DO IT AGAIN, FELLAS.

THIS IS **JERRY JUHL**, WHO WRITES FOR THE MUPPETS,

DON SAHLIN, WHO HELPS BUILD THE MUPPETS,

AND **FRANK OZ**, WHO WILL BE THE VOICE AND PERFORMER OF **GROVER**... AND EVEN **YODA**.

WHO'S YODA?

DON'T RUIN THE ENDING.

We did commercials, and performed on other shows.

But like so much of life, it was all just training for our next adventure.

Two TV producers named Joan Ganz Cooney and Jon Stone were about to give me the opportunity of a lifetime.

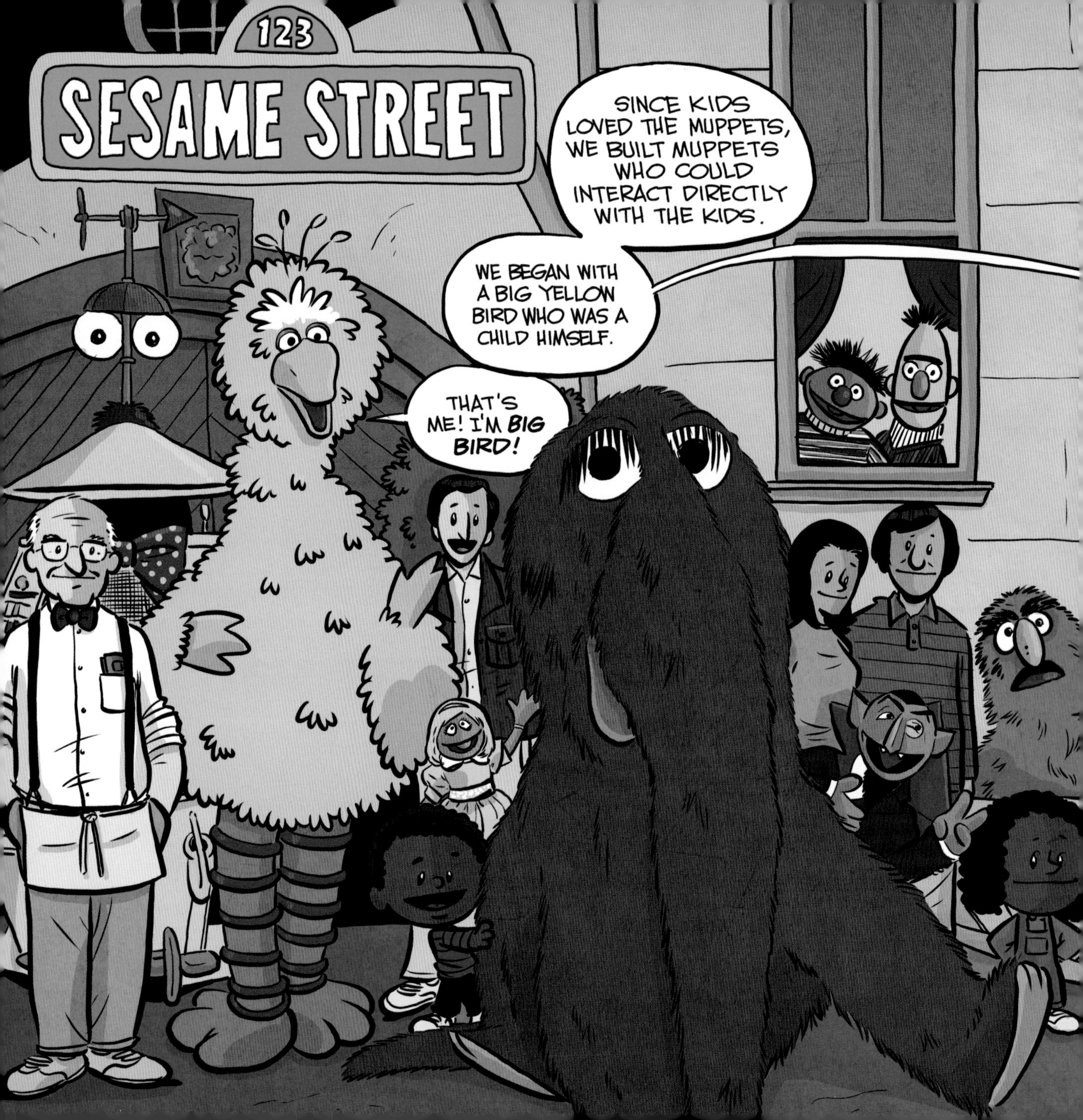
123
SESAME STREET
SINCE KIDS LOVED THE MUPPETS, WE BUILT MUPPETS WHO COULD INTERACT DIRECTLY WITH THE KIDS.
WE BEGAN WITH A BIG YELLOW BIRD WHO WAS A CHILD HIMSELF.
THAT'S ME! I'M BIG BIRD!

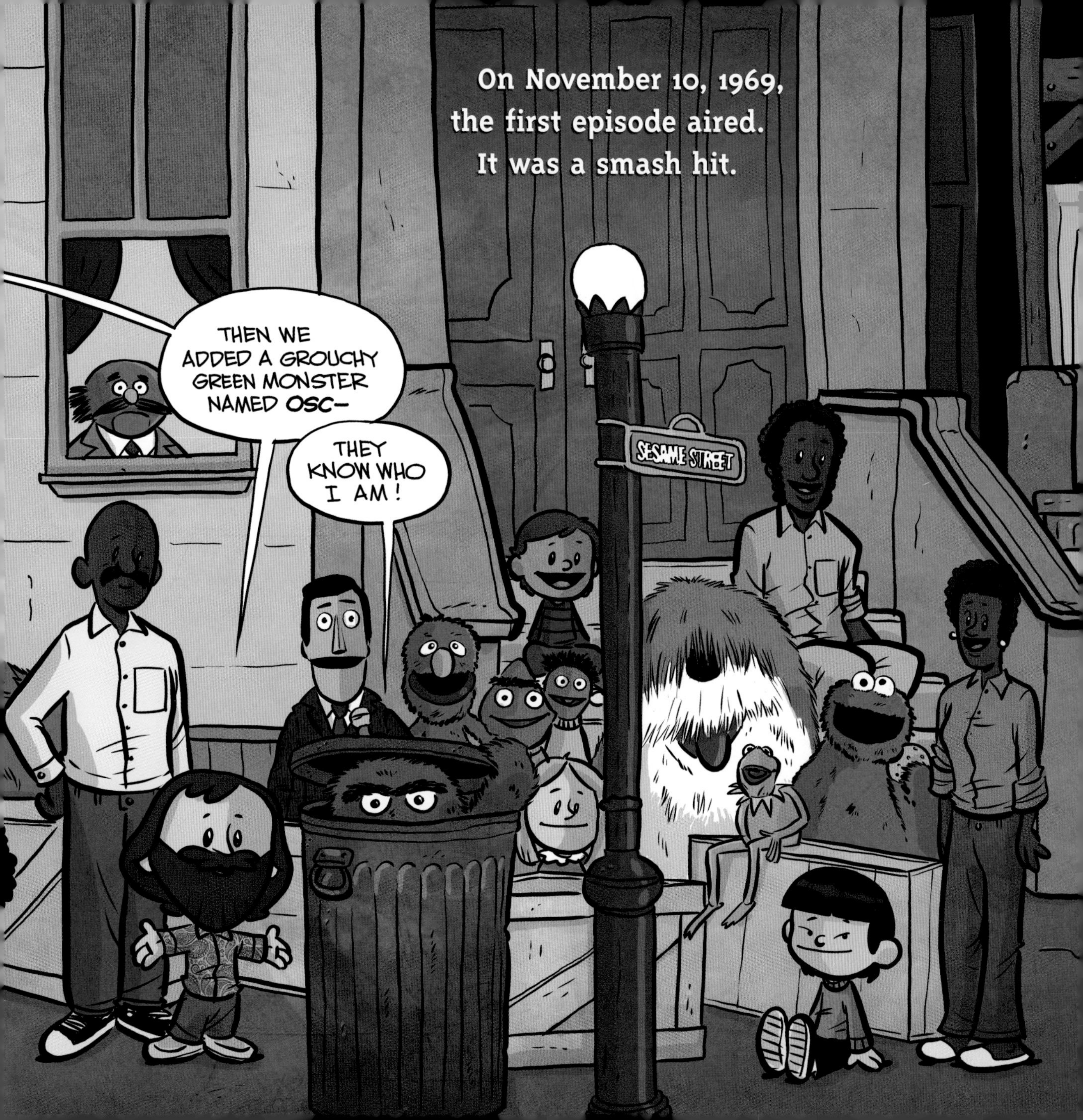
On November 10, 1969, the first episode aired. It was a smash hit.
THEN WE ADDED A GROUCHY GREEN MONSTER NAMED OSC—
THEY KNOW WHO I AM!
SESAME STREET

Every episode, *Sesame Street* taught the ABCs...

C IS FOR COOKIE!

and 123s.

THAT'S *FOUR!* FOUR BEAUTIFUL— AH AH AH — BATS!

It was one of the first shows to have kids of different races playing and learning together.

It taught kids how to share, how to take turns, and how to get along.

Certainly, with all its zany creatures, it made us laugh.

But at its best, with songwriters like Joe Raposo, *Sesame Street* made us *think*—especially about what kind of people we wanted to be.

GREEN'S THE COLOR OF SPRING

AND GREEN CAN BE COOL AND FRIENDLY-LIKE

AND GREEN CAN BE BIG LIKE AN OCEAN

OR IMPORTANT LIKE A MOUNTAIN

OR TALL LIKE A TREE.

Through song, the whole world heard that green—and all of us—can be anything.

Isn't it beautiful to see the world like that?

In fact, Kermit's humor never came from making fun of people; it came from bringing us together.

By focusing on the good in everyone, my own sense of wonder took over and my dream of entertaining others came true.

The Muppets and I went on new adventures.
And got to bring along some favorite old friends.

IT'S THE MUPPET SHOW, WITH OUR VERY SPECIAL GUEST STAR... MR. EDGAR BERGEN!

Every week on *The Muppet Show*, frogs, pigs, bears, and creatures of all kinds reminded the world that despite all the chaos—

CHAOS! CHAOS!

Sorry about that, folks.

As I was saying . . . On *The Muppet Show* and on *Sesame Street*, I wanted our audience to know that despite all the chaos, and despite our differences, there is nothing more fun than being together.

From there, I never stopped creating and dreaming.

In fact, the more we performed . . .

... the more fun we had, and the more my dream grew,
bringing millions of people together.
What can possibly be more magical than that?

. . . the more fun we had, and the more my dream grew,
bringing millions of people together.
What can possibly be more magical than that?

Sorry about that, folks.

As I was saying . . . On *The Muppet Show* and on *Sesame Street*, I wanted our audience to know that despite all the chaos, and despite our differences, there is nothing more fun than being together.

From there, I never stopped creating and dreaming.

In fact, the more we performed . . .

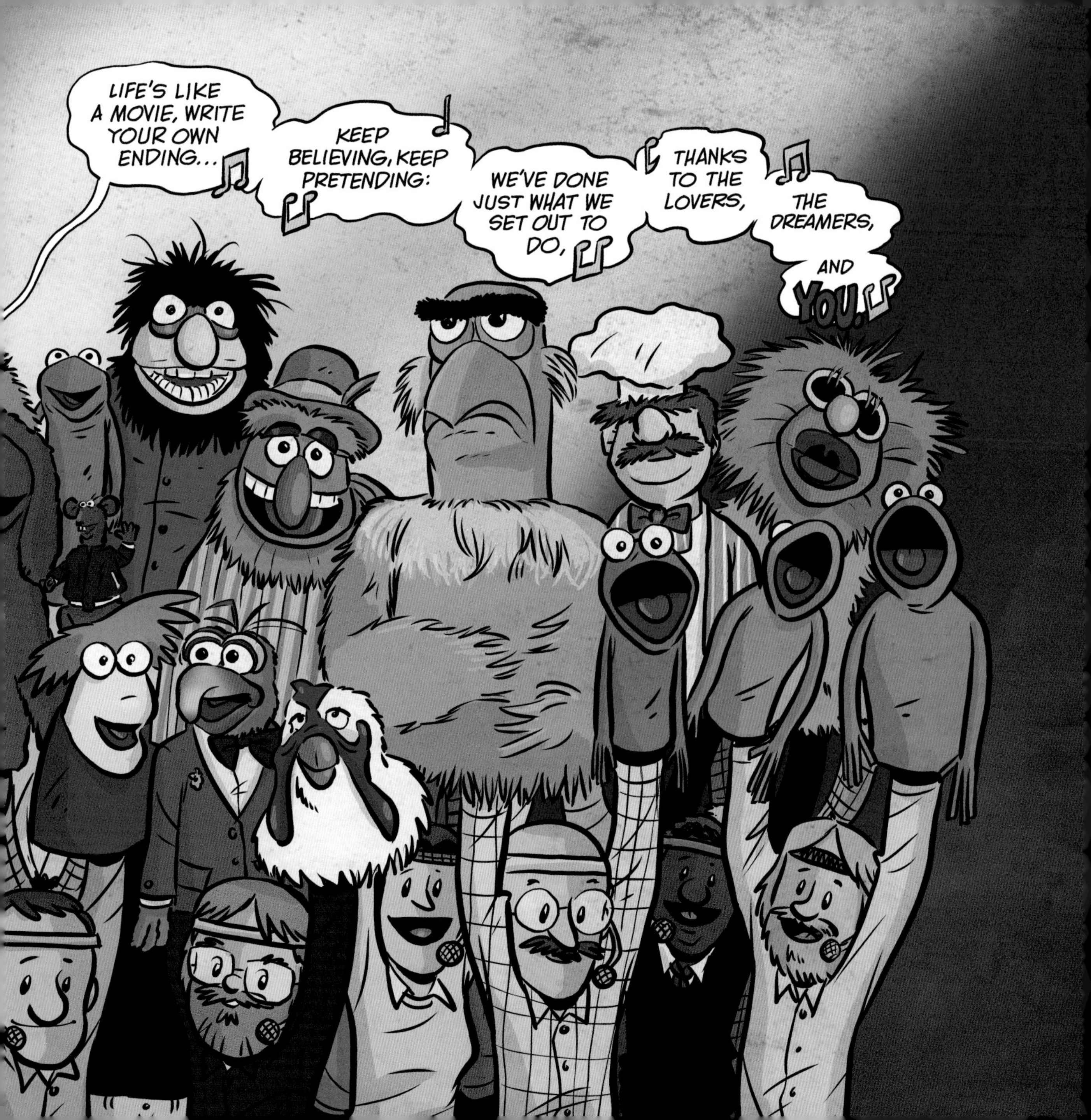
LIFE'S LIKE A MOVIE, WRITE YOUR OWN ENDING...
KEEP BELIEVING, KEEP PRETENDING:
WE'VE DONE JUST WHAT WE SET OUT TO DO,
THANKS TO THE LOVERS,
THE DREAMERS,
AND
YOU.

In my life, I loved to create.
But the secret behind my best creations wasn't
a strong hand, or a catchy song, or even a funny voice.
It was a simple idea: There's good in all of us.
Sure, we're all different. Some of us have beards,
or no hair, or blue fur, or green flippers.
But goodness lives within each of us.

That's an idea that should never get old.
Believe in the good of the world.
Create something new. Share what you love.
And find others who believe in those favorite
things you dream about.
Together . . .

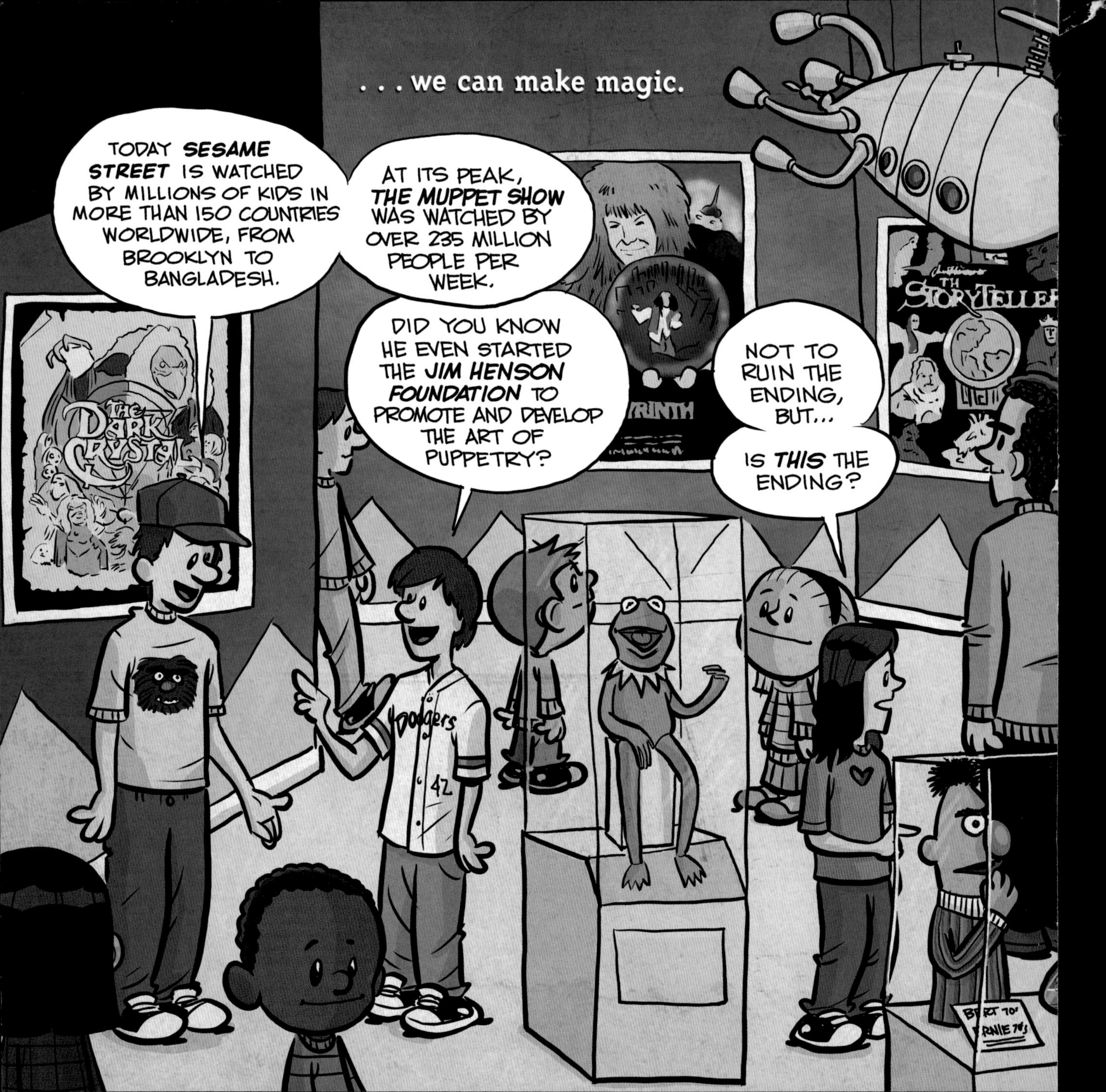
. . . we can make magic.
TODAY SESAME STREET IS WATCHED BY MILLIONS OF KIDS IN MORE THAN 150 COUNTRIES WORLDWIDE, FROM BROOKLYN TO BANGLADESH.
AT ITS PEAK, THE MUPPET SHOW WAS WATCHED BY OVER 235 MILLION PEOPLE PER WEEK.
DID YOU KNOW HE EVEN STARTED THE JIM HENSON FOUNDATION TO PROMOTE AND DEVELOP THE ART OF PUPPETRY?
NOT TO RUIN THE ENDING, BUT...
IS THIS THE ENDING?
The Dark Crystal
Dodgers
42

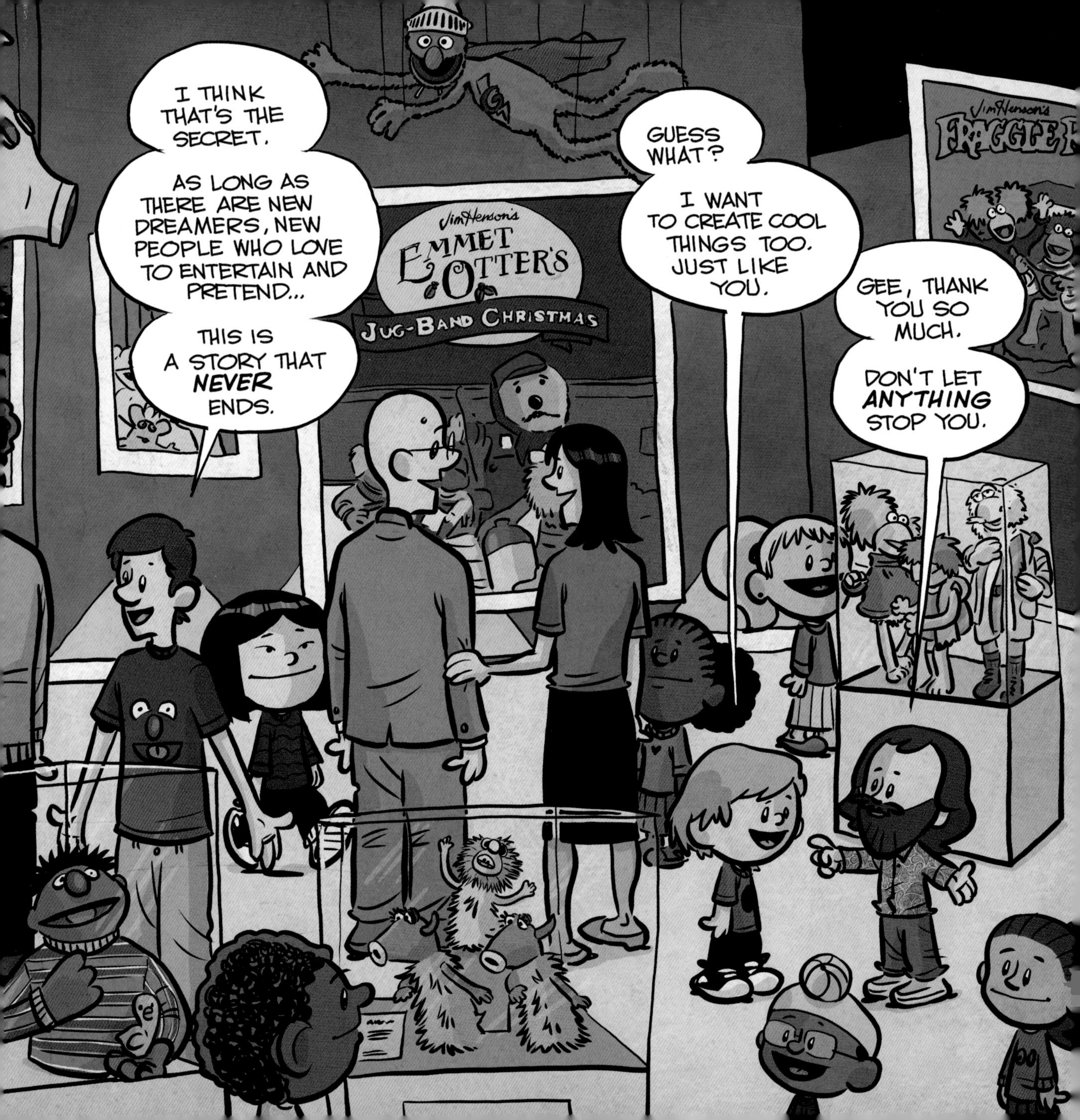

I THINK THAT'S THE SECRET.
AS LONG AS THERE ARE NEW DREAMERS, NEW PEOPLE WHO LOVE TO ENTERTAIN AND PRETEND...
THIS IS A STORY THAT **NEVER** ENDS.
Jim Henson's EMMET OTTER'S JUG-BAND CHRISTMAS
GUESS WHAT?
I WANT TO CREATE COOL THINGS TOO. JUST LIKE YOU.
Jim Henson's
GEE, THANK YOU SO MUCH.
DON'T LET **ANYTHING** STOP YOU.

It starts when we're kids.
That's when we learn some of the best things in life.
Laughing. Sharing. Imagining. Dreaming. Creating.
Never stop doing them.
And never stop being kind.
There's nothing wrong with being a do-gooder.

I am Jim Henson, and I will
keep believing and keep pretending.

"I've got a dream too, but it's about singing and dancing and making people happy. That's the kind of dream that gets better the more people you share it with." —Kermit the Frog

Timeline

SEPTEMBER 24, 1936	1954	1955	1955	MAY 28, 1959
Born in Greenville, MS	First television appearance (on *The Junior Morning Show* in Washington, DC)	*Sam and Friends* premieres	Makes first Kermit Muppet	Marries Jane Nebel

Young Jim as
snake charmer

Jim and Jane
with *Sam and
Friends* puppets

Frank Oz and Jim with
Miss Piggy and Kermit

The original
Sesame Street
cast with
puppeteers

1969	1974	1976	1977	1979	1983	MAY 16, 1990
Sesame Street premieres	The Muppets of *Sesame Street* win first Emmy Award	*The Muppet Show* premieres	*Emmet Otter's Jug Band Christmas* premieres	*The Muppet Movie* premieres	*Fraggle Rock* premieres	Dies in New York City

For Theo,
my dreamer.
This book isn't just for you;
it's about you.
May you always keep believing and keep pretending.
I'll be the one clapping.

—B.M.

For Jodi Gross.
The person who got me through college sane.
The person who could always make me laugh.
The person who did the best Kermit imitation.

—C.E.

For historical accuracy, we used Jim Henson's actual dialogue whenever possible. For more of Mr. Henson's true voice, we recommend and acknowledge the below titles. Special thanks to Cheryl Henson, a dear friend who amazes us, Lisa Henson, and Karen Falk, the Archives Director of The Jim Henson Company, for their input on early drafts. Special thanks to good pal Nick Raposo for letting us use his dad's beautiful song, "Bein' Green." It still inspires all of us here. Also, thanks to *Sesame Workshop* and *Muppet Studios*, for letting us use our favorite jokes.

· ·

SOURCES
Jim Henson: The Biography by Brian Jay Jones (Thanks, Brian!) (Ballantine, 2013)
Imagination Illustrated: The Jim Henson Journal by Karen Falk (Chronicle, 2012)
Street Gang: The Complete History of Sesame Street by Michael Davis (Viking, 2008)
It's Not Easy Being Green: And Other Things to Consider by Jim Henson, The Muppets, and Friends (Kingswell, 2005)
Jim Henson: The Works by Christopher Finch (Random House, 1993)
1982 interview with Judy Harris, *Cinefantastique* magazine (April/May 1983)
Henson.com/JimsRedBook

FURTHER READING FOR KIDS
Who Was Jim Henson? by Joan Holub (Grosset & Dunlap, 2010)
Jim Henson: The Guy Who Played with Puppets by Kathleen Krull (Random House, 2011)
The Muppets Character Encyclopedia (DK Publishing, 2014)

· ·

To learn more, please visit The Jim Henson Collection at the Center for Puppetry Arts in Atlanta and The Jim Henson Exhibition at the Museum of The Moving Image in New York.

DIAL BOOKS FOR YOUNG READERS
An imprint of Penguin Random House LLC, New York

First published in the United States of America by Dial Books for Young Readers, an imprint of Penguin Random House LLC, 2017
Text copyright © 2017 by Forty-four Steps, Inc. • Illustrations copyright © 2017 by Christopher Eliopoulos
"Sesame Workshop"®, "Sesame Street"®, and associated characters, trademarks, and design elements are owned and licensed by Sesame Workshop. © 2017 Sesame Workshop. All Rights Reserved.
The Muppets characters © Disney

Dial and Colophon is a registered trademark of Penguin Random House LLC. • Visit us online at penguinrandomhouse.com

Library of Congress Cataloging-in-Publication Data
Names: Meltzer, Brad, author. | Eliopoulos, Chris, illustrator. | Title: I am Jim Henson / Brad Meltzer ; illustrated by Christopher Eliopoulos. | Description: New York : Dial Books for Young Readers, an imprint of Penguin Group, [2017] | Series: Ordinary people change the world | Identifiers: LCCN 2016011350 | ISBN 9780525428503 (hardcover) | Subjects: LCSH: Henson, Jim—Juvenile literature. | Puppeteers—United States—Biography—Juvenile literature. | Television producers and directors—United States—Biography—Juvenile literature. | Muppet show (Television program)—Juvenile literature. | Classification: LCC PN1982.H46 M45 2017 | DDC 791.5/3092 [B] —dc23 LC record available at https://lccn.loc.gov/2016011350

"Bein' Green" lyrics on page 27 by Joe Raposo • Photos courtesy of The Jim Henson Company • Printed in China • 10 9 8 7 6 5
Designed by Jason Henry • Text set in Triplex • The artwork for this book was created digitally.

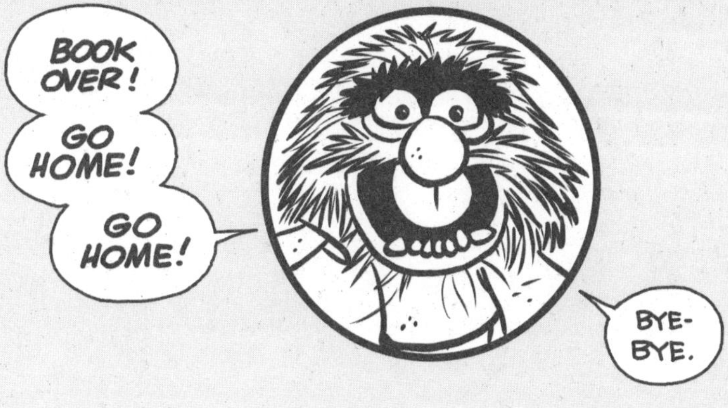
BOOK OVER!
GO HOME!
GO HOME!
BYE-BYE.

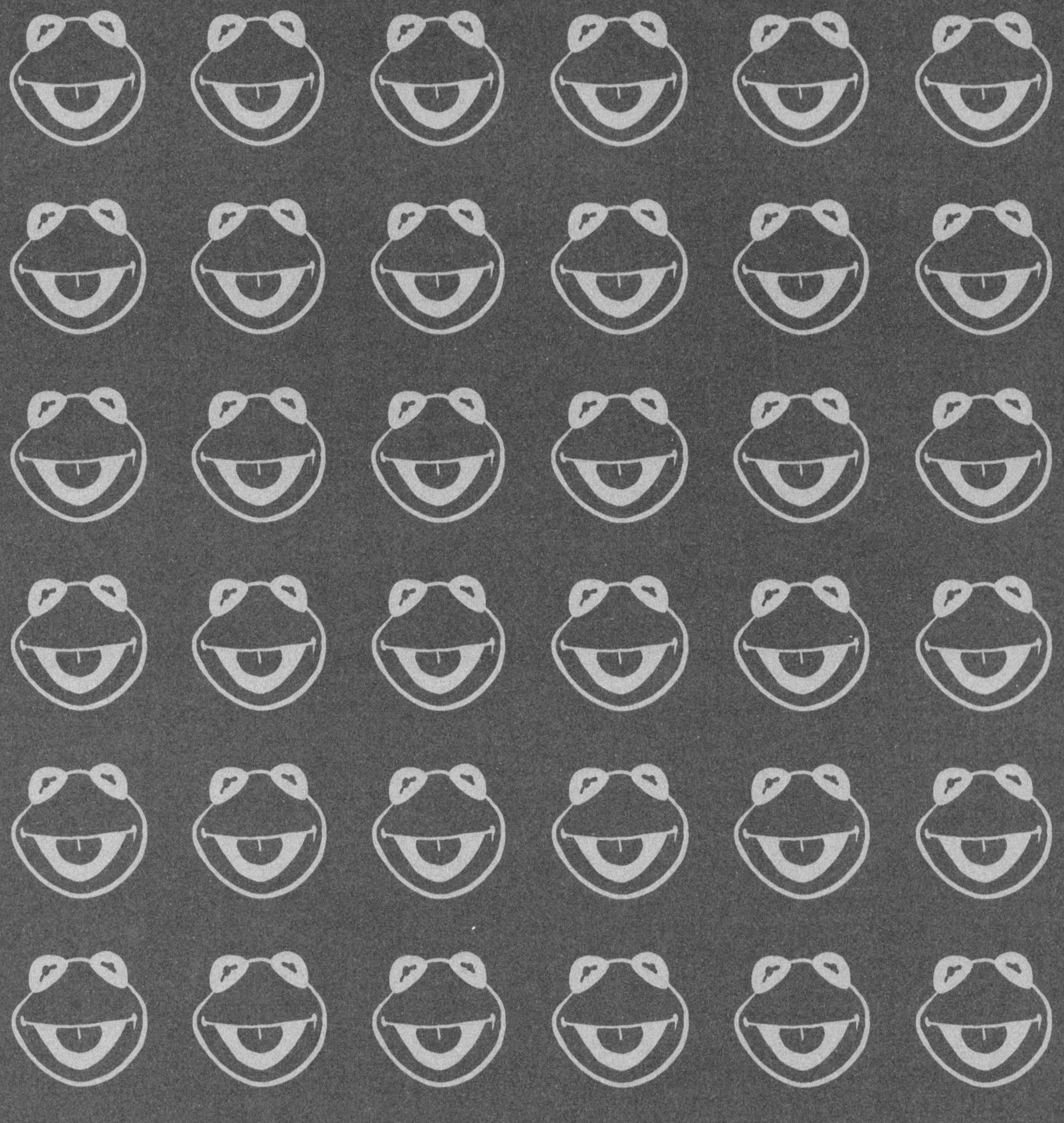